# Solar System Sights

Heera Kang

## Contents

**Rigby**
A Harcourt Achieve Imprint

www.Rigby.com
1-800-531-5015

# 1 A Sight in the Sky

It is a crisp winter night outside of Fairbanks, Alaska. The snow-covered spruce trees and mountain tops form an uneven horizon as you gaze out your bedroom window and into the night. You are conducting an observation for your Sky Gazers Club. The other members, who live all over the world, are waiting for your report of the events that are about to happen.

The sky is dark and clear when suddenly it lights up in a display of green, red, and white! These lights seem to roll and stretch across the sky. You stand in awe, staring out into space, and you think about what caused this natural fireworks display in the sky—and what is happening out there beyond the skies above Alaska.

You have just witnessed an **aurora**, a common sight in your Alaskan hometown. You close the curtains and sit down at your computer to write an e-mail to your fellow Sky Gazers, thinking about how you will describe this incredible sight. As you begin to explain the aurora to someone who has never seen one, you start to wonder more about the objects in the sky that are familiar to everyone, starting right here with Earth.

# Earth

From far away the planet Earth looks like a bright blue ball with white swirls of clouds. While there are several other planets close to ours, Earth is the only planet we know of that contains life. You are one of over 6.5 billion people on this planet, and there are countless forms of plant and animal life. About three-quarters of our planet is covered with water, and the land features range from high, jagged mountains to low plains and deserts.

# 2 Star Light, Star Bright

The sun that rises and sets every day in the sky above Earth is actually a star—a huge ball of burning gas that gives off energy. It looks larger than other stars we see in the sky because it is much closer to us than the others. Earth is constantly moving around, or **orbiting,** the sun in a regular path. We need the sun's energy and heat, which come to us in the form of light. The sun fuels all life on Earth.

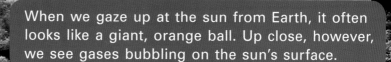

When we gaze up at the sun from Earth, it often looks like a giant, orange ball. Up close, however, we see gases bubbling on the sun's surface.

# The Sun and Our Seasons

The sun creates the four seasons we experience on Earth—winter, spring, summer, and fall. It takes Earth about 365 days to orbit the sun, which is equal to one Earth year. Earth also spins, or **rotates,** while it orbits the sun. Imagine a pole going through the center of Earth from north to south. That imaginary pole is Earth's **axis.** One turn on this axis takes 24 hours—one Earth day. The axis is tilted slightly, which creates the seasons we experience on Earth.

winter

spring

Because Earth is tilted, sometimes the top half of Earth—the northern hemisphere—is closer to the sun. This means that it is summer in the northern hemisphere. During this time, the bottom half of Earth—the southern hemisphere—is farther from the sun, and it is winter in that part of the world.

fall

summer

The sun doesn't just create the seasons of the year, for it can also tell us the time of day. Tomorrow the local members of your Sky Gazers Club are meeting at the library at 1:00 to discuss the aurora. What would you do if you didn't have a watch or a clock to tell you that it was almost time for your meeting? How would you know when to go to the library?

Before watches and clocks were invented, people marked the passing of time by observing the movement of the sun. They saw that the sun would rise and fall regularly in the sky and that they could use an instrument called a *sundial* to tell time. A sundial uses the shadows made by the sun to tell what time it is. You can make a sundial to see how people kept track of time long ago.

## Materials

- piece of cardboard (12" x 12")
- rocks or paperweights to hold down cardboard
- ball of clay
- thin straw (about 4 inches long)
- compass

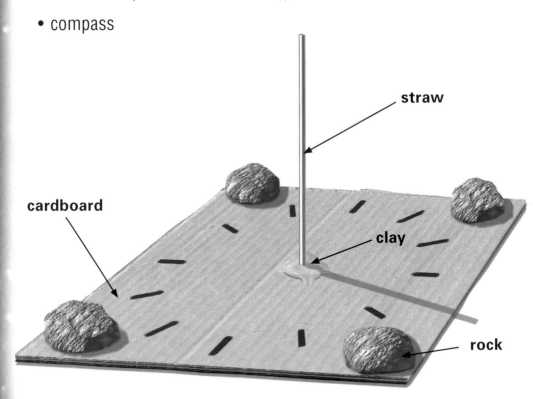

straw

cardboard

clay

rock

1. Make 12 marks in a circle on the cardboard with equal spacing between each mark.

2. Push the straw into the ball of clay so that the straw is pointing straight up.

3. Place the clay in the middle of the cardboard, making sure the straw is still pointing straight up.

4. Use your compass to find which direction is north. To do this, place the compass on the piece of cardboard and rotate the compass until the arrow points to the letter *N*. Draw an arrow pointing north on the piece of cardboard and label it with the letter *N*.

5. Place your sundial outside in the sun, on a flat surface, facing north. Use the rocks to hold down the corners of the base, so that the wind doesn't blow it away.

6. Starting early in the morning, observe the shadow that the straw makes on the cardboard. When the sun is at its highest point in the sky, it is noon. Label this point on your sundial "12" and number the rest of the points like the numbers on a clock. Now you can use your sundial to tell time!

# 3 The Magnificent Moon

The moon might look like the biggest shape in the night sky, yet Earth is still more than three times larger than the moon. You may have noticed lighter and darker spots on the moon's surface that make it look like a face. These areas are made up of big holes called *craters*. The lighter areas are also made up of mountains, and the darker spots are smooth, flat areas within some of the craters. Unlike the sun, the moon does not produce any light on its own. The glow we see from the moon is actually a reflection of light from the sun.

The moon is a familiar sight to everyone in your Sky Gazers Club, but do you know what it does? The moon is Earth's constant companion. It orbits Earth about once every 28 days, and it affects us in ways we might not even realize. Have you ever wondered what makes the waves on beaches flow in and out? The ocean's **tides**—the rise and fall of the ocean waters—are controlled by the moon.

sun

moon

Earth

# The Moon and Our Tides

Everything in space, including the moon, the sun, and Earth, has a force that pulls things toward it. This force is called **gravity.** As the moon orbits Earth, the moon's gravity affects things on Earth, including the water in our oceans. The moon's gravity pushes and pulls the ocean water, which creates the waves we see at the beach. The sun also has gravity, so it pulls at our ocean waters as the Earth moves around the sun.

Remember that the moon is constantly orbiting Earth, and Earth is constantly orbiting the sun. The forces of gravity are strongest on the area of Earth that is directly beneath the moon and on the area that is farthest away from the moon. At this point, tides in both of these places will be at their highest. The next time you hear that it is high tide, you will know that you are either directly beneath the moon or in an area very far away from it.

gravitational pull

# The Phases of the Moon

Did you notice the shape of the moon last night? If not, check it tonight. The shape of the moon in your night sky is the result of the positions of Earth, the moon, and the sun. Half of the moon is always lit by the sun, but because the moon and Earth are always in orbit, we don't always see the half of the moon that is lit. The shape of the moon in our sky is the part of the moon that is lit by the sun when viewed from Earth.

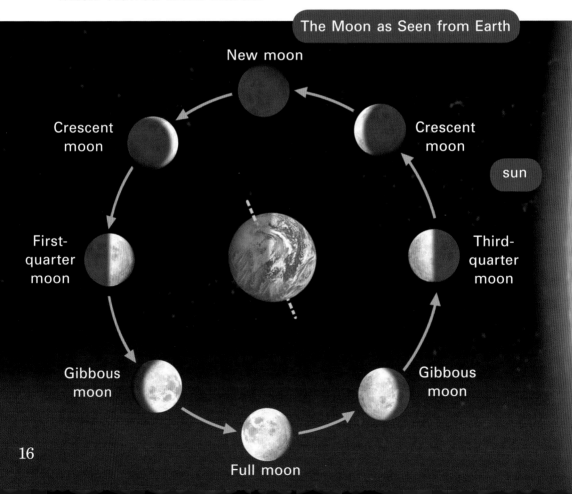

The Moon as Seen from Earth

New moon

Crescent moon

Crescent moon

sun

First-quarter moon

Third-quarter moon

Gibbous moon

Gibbous moon

Full moon

**New moon:** The moon is lined up between Earth and the sun. The side of the moon that is lit by the sun is not facing us, so we see no moon at all.

**Crescent moon:** As the moon moves away from the sun, we see a bit more of the sunlit side of the moon each night. After a few days, we begin to see a thin, curved shape in the sky. This shape is called a *crescent.*

**First-quarter moon:** The crescent moon appears to grow each night. When we see half of the moon in the sky, we call it first-quarter moon because the moon has traveled one-quarter of its orbit around Earth.

**Gibbous moon:** We continue to see more of the moon. When we see more than half of the entire moon in the sky, it is a shape we call gibbous.

**Full moon:** The moon has now come to a place where we can see its full shape. We call this phase the full moon. The full moon rises when the sun sets, and it sets just as the sun rises. The moon has now traveled half of its orbit.

**Gibbous moon:** During the second half of the moon's orbit around Earth, the moon appears to grow thinner. The first phase after the full moon is the gibbous moon again.

**Third-quarter moon:** When we can see half of the moon again, it is called the third-quarter moon. We are seeing the other side of the moon from when it was in the first quarter phase. We call this the third-quarter moon because it is three-quarters of the way through its path around Earth.

**Crescent moon:** As the moon continues its orbit, it appears to grow thinner still into another crescent shape. Finally, it goes into the new moon phase again, and we do not see it in the sky.

# 4 What Else Is out There?

As you think about the sun and the moon, you return to your window and peer through your telescope. You remember that in addition to Earth, there are other planets that orbit the sun at different distances. Although we might feel differently on days that are very hot or very cold, Earth is the perfect distance from the sun for us to survive. However, the conditions on the other planets are so extreme that life on those planets is impossible.

Saturn's rings

Jupiter

Earth

Mercury

Venus  Mars

sun

Saturn

Uranus

Neptune

The planet Mercury is closest to the sun. On Mercury temperatures can soar to over 700° F and dip down to below -200° F in the same day!

The second planet from the sun, Venus, is about the same size as Earth, but that is where the similarity ends. The air on Venus is poisonous to living things, and temperatures can reach more than 800° F.

Earth is the third planet from the sun, and after Earth is Mars. Mars has canyons deeper than the Grand Canyon and mountains taller than the highest peak on Earth. Like Venus, Mars is very cold. The temperature on Mars never climbs higher than -10° F.

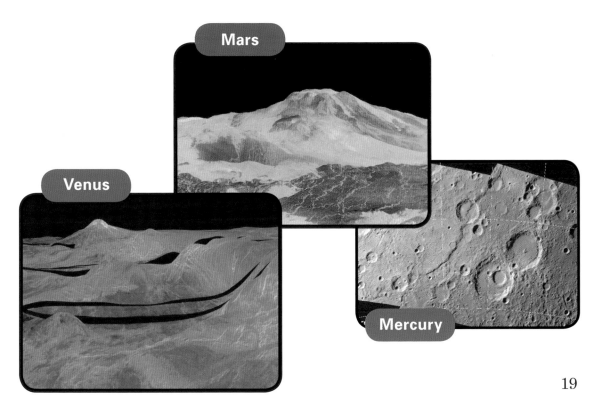

Mars

Venus

Mercury

Next in line are the planets Jupiter, Saturn, Uranus, and Neptune. These planets are much bigger than Mercury, Venus, Earth, and Mars. They also all have rings made of materials such as dust and rocks. However, Saturn and Neptune also have pieces of ice floating in their rings.

Pluto is farthest from the sun. People used to believe that Pluto was the smallest planet, but now Pluto is not considered to be a planet. We don't know much about Pluto because it is so far away, but we do know that the surface probably consists mostly of rock and ice.

Together, the sun and the planets that orbit it form the **solar system.**

### Planet Pluto?

Pluto was discovered in 1930. Pluto is made of rock and ice and orbits the sun in an oval path. Scientists have discovered almost 100 objects that look like icy versions of Pluto. These objects are part of the Kuiper Belt, a group of objects orbiting the sun. After much debate, scientists and astronomers decided that Pluto is not a planet.

# The Universe

As you look through your telescope, you are amazed by another sight in the night sky: stars—more you could ever count. Along with the other objects in our solar system, billions of stars make up our **galaxy,** the Milky Way. The vastness of space doesn't end there. The Milky Way is only one of many other galaxies in what we call the **universe.** The universe stretches farther than scientists can tell.

## Sky Gazer's Notes on the Universe

- Mercury, Venus, Earth, Mars, Jupiter, Saturn, Uranus, and Neptune are the planets that orbit the sun, which is a giant star.
- Like the sun, other stars can have planets orbiting around them. Some of these planets may also have moons.
- A galaxy has hundreds of billions of stars swirling around it. Our galaxy is the Milky Way.
- The universe is made up of many galaxies.

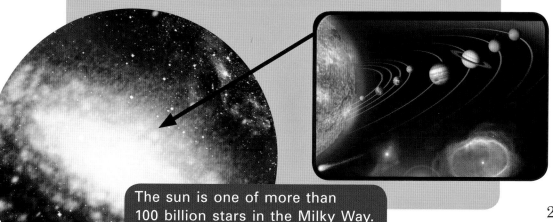

The sun is one of more than 100 billion stars in the Milky Way.

# 5 Awesome Auroras

You return to your computer to write your e-mail to your fellow Sky Gazers and see that you have received a message from one of them instead! This one comes from a Sky Gazer in New Zealand, another place where auroras can be seen regularly.

**From:** SkyWatcher@NewZealand.sun
**To:** SkyGazers@universe.sky
**Subject:** Sights in the Sky

Dear Sky Gazers,

The sky overhead is a brilliant painting, glowing with color. The aurora is shining brilliantly. Rays of white light shoot out from the horizon and reflect on the glittering waters of the South Pacific Ocean. Distant stars sparkle behind the colors, and the effect is like a fireworks show in the sky.

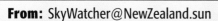

# What Is an Aurora?

The lights of auroras we see from here on Earth are caused by the sun. The sun is made up of gases. These gases are extremely hot, so the surface of the sun is a fiery mixture of boiling gases. Think of a pot of boiling water. When the water gets hot and boils rapidly, sometimes the water will spout out from the bubbles. In the same way, the gas on the sun will boil and spout out particles into space. These particles are very small, yet they travel far enough to reach Earth. The glow of auroras results from the interaction between the sun's particles and the gases that surround Earth, creating a brilliant light show in the sky.

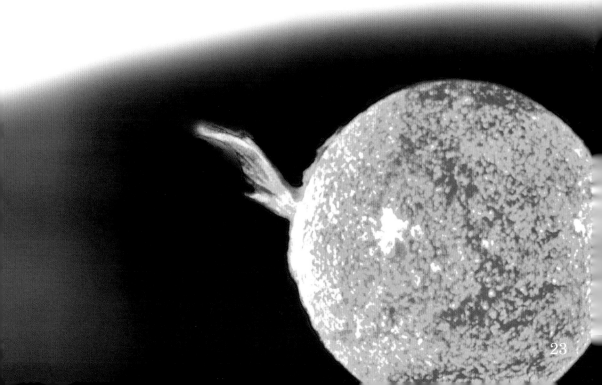

# Protecting Earth

These eruptions from the sun would be extremely destructive to Earth, but, fortunately, Earth is surrounded by the **atmosphere**, which is a thin layer of gases. This layer of gases protects us from most of the sun's harmful effects, letting in all of the sun's life-giving light. Without the atmosphere, temperatures would soar to dangerous levels, as they do on Mercury and Venus, and we would not be protected from chemicals produced by the sun. The **ozone layer** is part of Earth's atmosphere that protects life on Earth from harmful effects of the sun. Unfortunately, there is a massive hole in the ozone layer, which can create dangerous conditions.

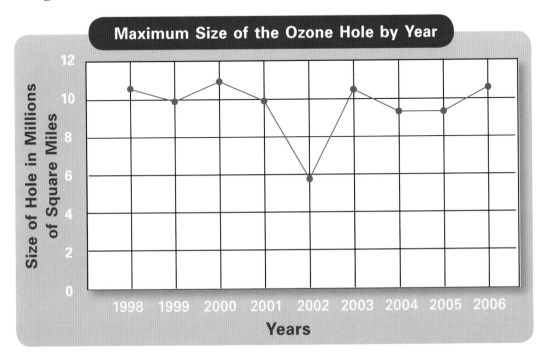

Maximum Size of the Ozone Hole by Year

# What's Happening to the Ozone Layer

Scientists first started studying the ozone layer in the early 1970s and found that this shield is slowly being damaged. Scientists found holes in the ozone layer resulting from a combination of cold weather and certain chemicals humans were putting into the air. Since then many people have stopped using these chemicals, and it is important that we be careful when choosing the products we will use. Scientists continue to watch the ozone layer closely to monitor the size of the hole.

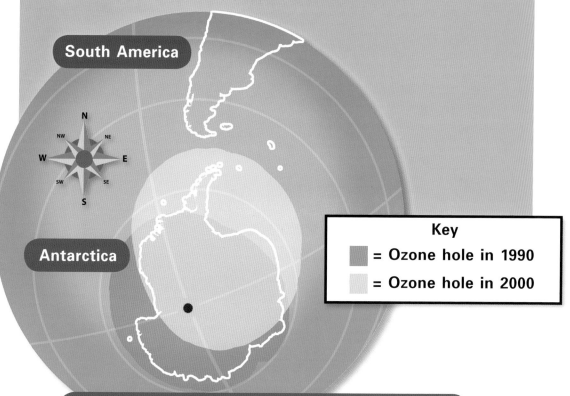

South America

N
NW    NE
W         E
SW    SE
S

Antarctica

**Key**

= Ozone hole in 1990

= Ozone hole in 2000

In 2000, the ozone hole over Antarctica reached its largest size ever: 10.9 million square miles. This is roughly twice the size of Antarctica.

# 6 Moon on the Move

## Lunar Eclipse

Thanks to your friend's detailed description of an aurora, you are now ready to write your own. Just as you begin, you hear the familiar beep from your computer telling you that you have another new e-mail message. This writer lives far away in South America.

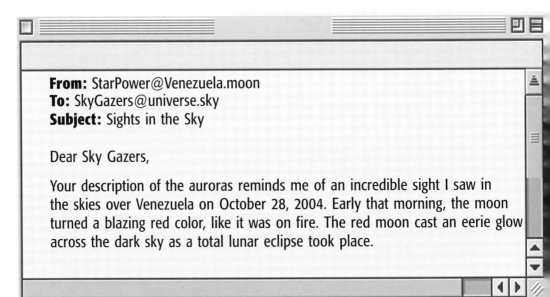

**From:** StarPower@Venezuela.moon
**To:** SkyGazers@universe.sky
**Subject:** Sights in the Sky

Dear Sky Gazers,

Your description of the auroras reminds me of an incredible sight I saw in the skies over Venezuela on October 28, 2004. Early that morning, the moon turned a blazing red color, like it was on fire. The red moon cast an eerie glow across the dark sky as a total lunar eclipse took place.

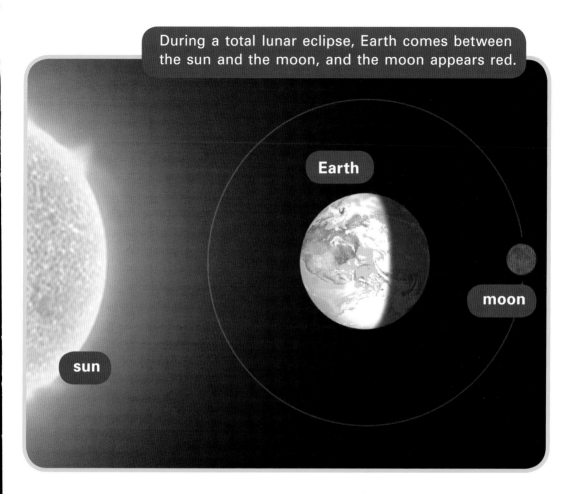

During a total lunar eclipse, Earth comes between the sun and the moon, and the moon appears red.

Earth

moon

sun

A total lunar eclipse occurs when Earth blocks sunlight from the moon. Remember that the moon itself doesn't give off any light. The glow of the moon is only a reflection of the sun's light. During a total lunar eclipse, the moon appears a dark red color as the light from the sun passes through Earth's atmosphere as it reaches the moon.

# Solar Eclipse

Just as you finish reading that message, another one pops up, this time from a Sky Gazer remembering another fantastic display in the sky.

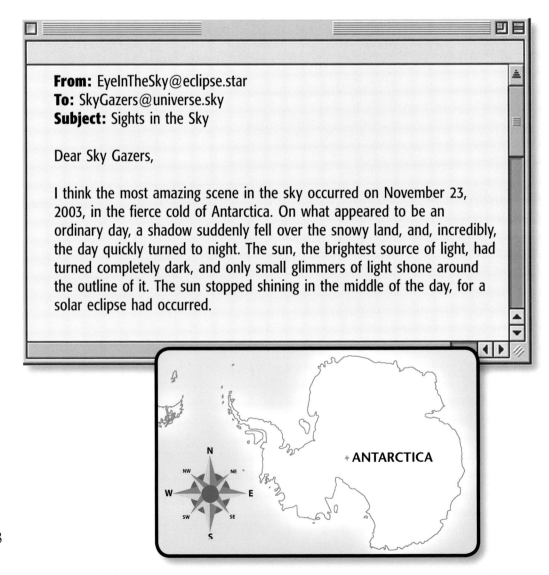

**From:** EyeInTheSky@eclipse.star
**To:** SkyGazers@universe.sky
**Subject:** Sights in the Sky

Dear Sky Gazers,

I think the most amazing scene in the sky occurred on November 23, 2003, in the fierce cold of Antarctica. On what appeared to be an ordinary day, a shadow suddenly fell over the snowy land, and, incredibly, the day quickly turned to night. The sun, the brightest source of light, had turned completely dark, and only small glimmers of light shone around the outline of it. The sun stopped shining in the middle of the day, for a solar eclipse had occurred.

ANTARCTICA

During a solar eclipse, the moon moves in between Earth and the sun. The moon is much smaller than the sun, but it is much closer to Earth. This is why it can block our view of something as large as the sun.

A total solar eclipse occurs when the moon blocks the light of the sun.

sun

moon

Earth

Think about it this way: Picture a basketball sitting on the floor of your school's gym. From the opposite end of the gym, you can see everything around the basketball. But if you were to hold the basketball in front of your eyes, it would block your view, and you wouldn't be able to see around it. In a solar eclipse, the moon acts like the basketball, and Earth is like your eyes. Because the moon is so close to Earth, we can't see around it, and it blocks our view of the sun during a solar eclipse.

The skies offer countless other sights for sky gazers around the world. With all of these vivid descriptions of amazing activities in the sky, you are finally ready to write your message to your fellow Sky Gazers.

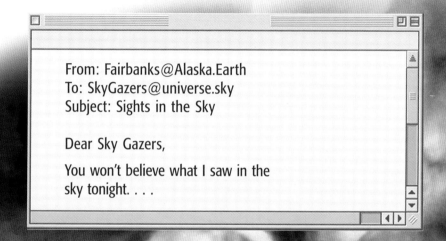

From: Fairbanks@Alaska.Earth
To: SkyGazers@universe.sky
Subject: Sights in the Sky

Dear Sky Gazers,

You won't believe what I saw in the sky tonight. . . .

## Glossary

**atmosphere** the thin layer of gases surrounding Earth and protecting it from harmful effects of the sun

**aurora** a stream of lights that occurs when particles from the sun reach a planet's atmosphere

**axis** the straight line around which a round object rotates

**galaxy** a large grouping of stars, gases, and dust

**gravity** a force that pulls two objects together

**orbit** to go around something in a regular path

**ozone layer** protective gases in Earth's atmosphere

**rotate** to turn around in one place

**solar system** the sun and the planets that orbit it

**tide** the rising and falling of the surface of ocean water caused by the gravity of the sun and moon

**universe** everything in space, including the solar system and all galaxies

## Index